Backyard Animals

Raccoons

Jennifer Hurtig

www.av2books.com

Go to www.av2books.com, and enter this book's unique code.

BOOK CODE

AV² by Weigl brings you media enhanced books that support active learning.

AV² provides enriched content that supplements and complements this book. Weigl's AV² books strive to create inspired learning and engage young minds in a total learning experience.

Your AV² Media Enhanced books come alive with...

Audio
Listen to sections of the book read aloud.

Key Words
Study vocabulary, and complete a matching word activity.

Video
Watch informative video clips.

Quizzes
Test your knowledge.

Embedded Weblinks
Gain additional information for research.

Slide Show
View images and captions, and prepare a presentation.

Try This!
Complete activities and hands-on experiments.

... and much, much more!

Published by AV² by Weigl
350 5th Avenue, 59th Floor
New York, NY 10118
Website: www.av2books.com www.weigl.com

Library of Congress Cataloging-in-Publication Data

Hurtig, Jennifer.
Raccoons / Jennifer Hurtig.
p. cm. -- (Backyard animals)
Includes index.
ISBN 978-1-61913-069-2 (hard cover : alk. paper) -- ISBN 978-1-61913-266-5 (soft cover : alk. paper)
1. Raccoon--Juvenile literature. I. Title.
QL737.C26H873 2013
599.76'32--dc23

2011044653

Printed in the United States of America in North Mankato, Minnesota
1 2 3 4 5 6 7 8 9 0 16 15 14 13 12

WEP060112
012012

Project Coordinator Karen Durrie
Art Director Terry Paulhus.

Every reasonable effort has been made to trace ownership and to obtain permission to reprint copyright material. The publishers would be pleased to have any errors or omissions brought to their attention so that they may be corrected in subsequent printings.

Photo Credits
Weigl acknowledges Getty Images as its primary photo supplier for this title.

Contents

Meet the Raccoon

Raccoons are medium-sized **mammals**. They have dark fur around their eyes that looks like a mask. There is white fur around the mask. Raccoons have a pointed snout and a bushy, ringed tail. They have gray or brown fur on their body.

Raccoons have five toes on each paw. They use their front paws like hands to grab and hold onto objects. Raccoons use their paws to climb trees. They are very good swimmers.

Raccoons are nocturnal. This means they are mainly active at night. They are very smart. Some raccoons can open garbage cans, jars, and latches.

Raccoons can climb down trees headfirst. They do this by turning their back feet so that their toes face backwards.

Baby raccoons live and travel with their family for up to one year before living on their own.

All about Raccoons

Raccoons belong to a group of tree-climbing mammals. This group is closely related to bears.

There are seven **species** of raccoon. They live in North, South, and Central America. Each place offers different food, climates, and **habitats**. Some types of raccoon are rare and are not found easily by people.

Raccoons search for food in streams. They use their paws to turn over rocks and small tree branches.

Where Raccoons Live

Bahaman Raccoon	Cozumel Island Raccoon
• Lives in the Bahamas	• Found on Mexico's Cozumel Island
Barbados Raccoon	**Crab-eating Raccoon**
• Once lived in Barbados • The last time one was seen by humans was in 1964	• Lives in marshy and jungle areas in Central and South America
Common Raccoon	
• Lives in Canada, the United States, and South America	• Often lives near humans
Guadeloupe Raccoon	**Tres Marias Raccoon**
• Lives on the Caribbean island of Guadeloupe	• Found on the Tres Marias Islands, near Mexico

Raccoon History

Little is known about when raccoons first appeared on Earth. Some people believe that early American Indians hunted raccoons for food and fur. Later, they traded raccoon **pelts** with Europeans.

Many settlers began to hunt raccoons. They wore "coonskin" hats that were made of raccoon fur. In the 1920s, raccoon skin coats became popular. Today, some people still hunt raccoons for their fur.

Sometimes, raccoons are trapped because they eat farmers' crops. Raccoons also are threatened by **predators,** a lack of food sources, and diseases such as rabies.

Raccoons communicate with each other by chirping, growling, crying, or hissing.

Raccoons are native to North and South America. People have taken them over to Europe and Asia.

Raccoon Shelter

Raccoons can be found in cities and towns. They live near trees and water. Most raccoons do not make their own homes. They live in buildings, hollow tree trunks, old nests, wood piles, hay stacks, or under objects. They may live in beaver lodges and coyote or badger dens that have been left empty.

Raccoons live in different climates. Some live in hot and humid forests. Others live farther north where the weather is colder. A raccoon that lives in a cold place has thicker fur than one that lives in a warm place.

Raccoons are not active in winter. They stay in dens for long periods of time when it is cold. In warm weather, raccoons lay on the ground or on tree branches.

Raccoons move to a new living space every few days, except when they are breeding or taking care of their young.

Raccoon Features

Raccoons have **adapted** to living in many different habitats. Thick fur keeps them warm in winter. The color of their fur helps raccoons hide from predators because it blends with their surroundings. Other parts of a raccoon's body have special features as well.

EARS AND EYES
Raccoons have excellent night vision and good hearing.

FEET
A raccoon's foot has claws on each of its five toes. Raccoons can spread their toes to grab food and other objects.

FUR

Raccoons have long fur that most often is a brownish-gray color. The darker fur around their eyes may help them to see better at night. It helps reduce the glare from any light sources.

TAIL

A raccoon's tail fur usually has five to seven dark circles. Raccoons use their tail for balance when they are climbing.

LEGS

A raccoon's back legs are longer than its front legs. Raccoons cannot run very fast. They waddle when they walk. However, they can swim and climb trees.

What Do Raccoons Eat?

Raccoons are **omnivores**. They eat insects, birds, eggs, fish, and young rabbits. They also eat fruits and vegetables, such as plums and corn. Near water, raccoons hunt for crayfish. They look for insects under rocks. Raccoons dig in gardens and pick at food in bird feeders.

The food raccoons eat changes with the seasons. In spring, raccoons mainly eat meat. In summer, they eat berries, nuts, and other plants. In autumn, raccoons eat more food than they do at other times of the year. They do this to prepare for winter. Raccoons eat corn, nuts, and grain to build fat. They use their stored fat to survive in cold weather when food is more difficult to find. During this time, up to half of the raccoon's body weight may be fat.

The scientific name for raccoons is *Procyon lotor*. This means "washer bear." Raccoons earned this name because they often dip their food in water.

Raccoons have sharp teeth that they use to eat meat. Raccoons also have strong back teeth that they use to eat other foods, such as fruits.

Raccoon Life Cycle

Most raccoons look for a mate in January or February. The mother will give birth about two months later. Raccoons that live in northern areas will have three to seven babies. In southern places, female raccoons have two to three babies. Baby raccoons are called cubs or kits.

Baby

A baby raccoon weighs less than 3 ounces (85 grams) when it is born. A raccoon cub's eyes do not open until a few weeks later. At birth, a cub's fur is light gray. It darkens in the following weeks. The mask appears when the cub is about 10 days old.

1 Month Old

At one month of age, a raccoon cub weighs 10 to 16 ounces (283 to 454 g). It can stand up. When cubs are two to three months old, they begin to hunt with their mother. She protects them from predators. Most raccoons stay with their mother for up to one year.

A female raccoon may stay with her **litter** until she has another one. Males live alone. They do not help raise the babies.

Adult

Adult raccoons can grow to be 3 feet (0.9 meters) long. Most raccoons weigh about 30 pounds (14 kilograms), but some can be almost 40 pounds (18 kg). Male raccoons are usually bigger than females. In nature, raccoons live for five to eight years.

Encountering Raccoons

When raccoons live near people, they can cause damage to gardens and spill trash cans. If a raccoon lives near your home, do not feed the animal. It is better to urge the raccoon to move to another place. Raccoons prefer to look for food in the dark. Turning on lights will annoy a raccoon.

People should not keep raccoons as pets. They often become **aggressive** as they age. If they are released into nature, they will not have the skills they need to survive.

Raccoons can get **parasites** and diseases such as roundworm or rabies. They can pass on these diseases to pets and humans.

Baby raccoons do not become nocturnal until they are nearly a year old. They often explore during the day without their mothers.

Raccoons may search through garbage for food. Bins that lock can keep raccoons out of garbage.

Myths and Legends

Stories and legends about raccoons often show the tricky side of this clever animal. Raccoons are curious animals. This sometimes leads them into trouble. Many American Indian legends describe the raccoon as a mischief maker that plays tricks on other animals and people.

The raccoon gets its name from the Algonquian Indian word *arakun*. This means "he scratches with his hands."

The Raccoon and the Blind Men

A version of this legend is part of many American Indian cultures.

Two old, blind men lived together. One day, they were cooking eight pieces of meat, four for each of them. The men each took one piece of meat to eat. A raccoon passing by decided to play a trick on the old men. He quietly picked out four pieces of cooked meat. Then, one of the men put his hand in the bowl to take another piece of meat. He found that there were only two pieces left. "My friend," he said to the other old man, "you must be very hungry to have gobbled up so much meat already."

The other replied, "I have not taken it. I think you have eaten it yourself." The two men began to argue. Raccoon was watching them, and he began to laugh. Then, he took the last two pieces of meat and left. Raccoon called back to the men.

"I have played a trick on you. You should not blame each other so easily."

Frequently Asked Questions

What sounds do raccoons make?

Answer: Raccoons make many different sounds. Their calls include chattering, whistling, growling, snorting, barking, and clicking their teeth.

How do raccoons spend the winter?

Answer: Raccoons are not very active in winter. They mainly stay in their den. They use up their fat when they cannot find food.

What should I do if I find an ill raccoon?

Answer: If you find an ill raccoon, you should call a veterinarian, or animal doctor, for help. Do not touch the animal.

Words to Know

adapted: adjusted to the natural environment

aggressive: behaving in an unfriendly manner

habitats: natural environments of living things

litter: a group of animals born to one mother at the same time

mammals: animals that have warm blood, hair or fur, and feed milk to their young

omnivores: animals that eat meat and plants

parasites: living things that live on or in other living things

pelts: skin of an animal with the fur still on it

predators: animals that hunt other animals for food

species: a group of living things that has many features in common

Index

Log on to www.av2books.com

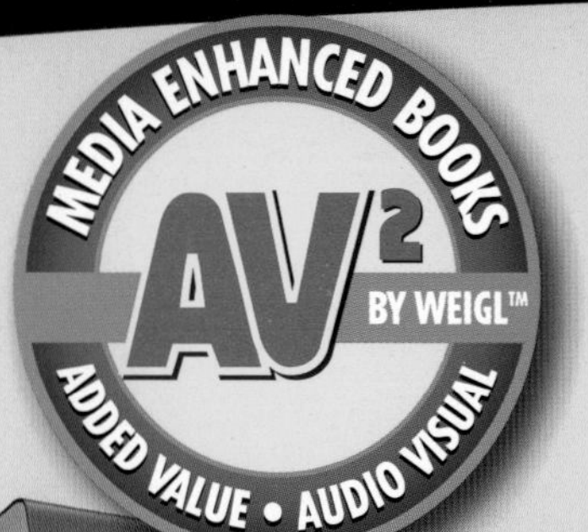

AV² by Weigl brings you media enhanced books that support active learning. Go to www.av2books.com, and enter the special code found on page 2 of this book. You will gain access to enriched and enhanced content that supplements and complements this book. Content includes video, audio, weblinks, quizzes, a slide show, and activities.

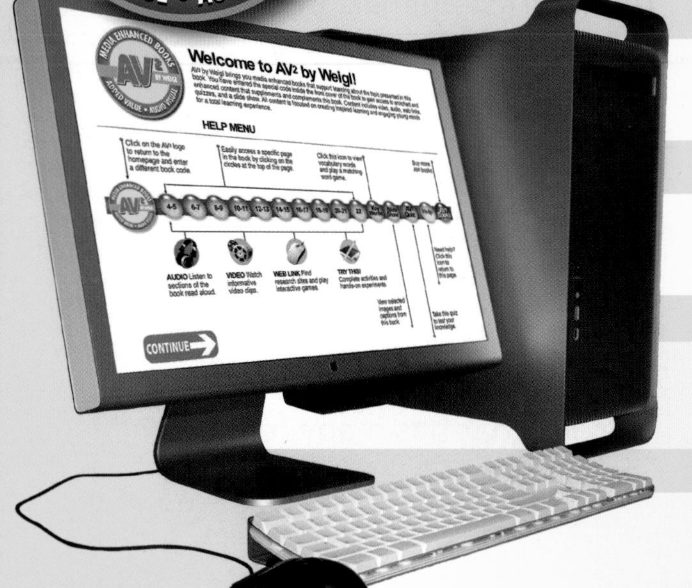

Audio
Listen to sections of the book read aloud.

Video
Watch informative video clips.

Embedded Weblinks
Gain additional information for research.

Try This!
Complete activities and hands-on experiments.

WHAT'S ONLINE?

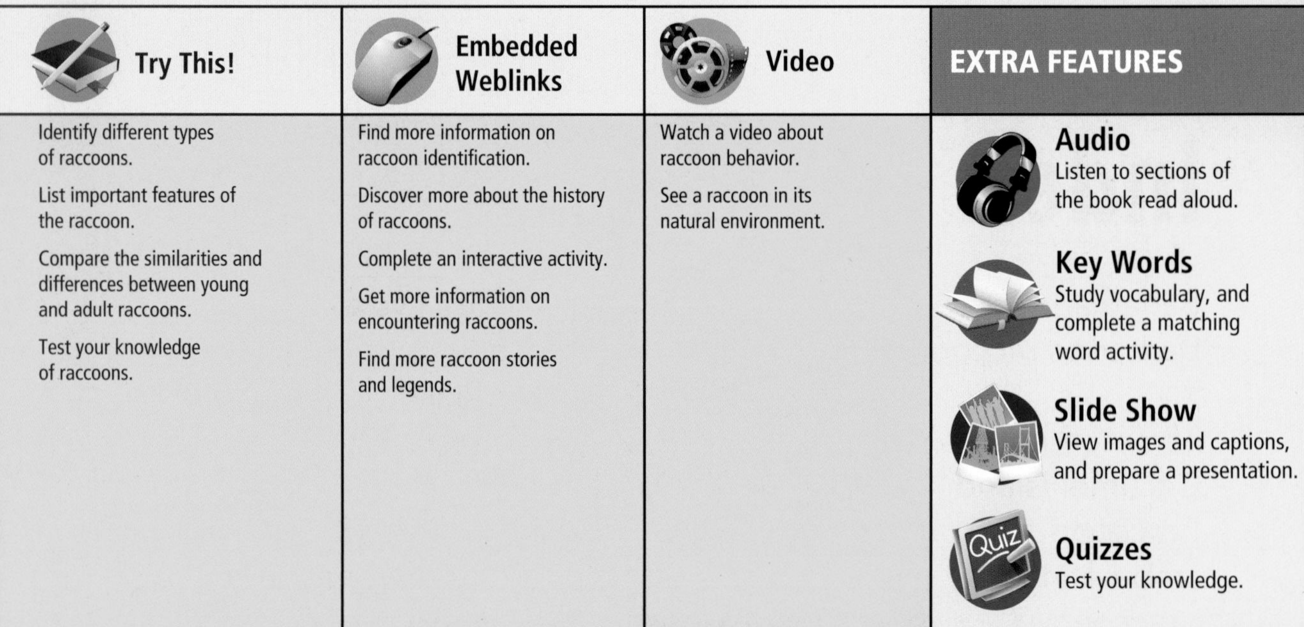

Try This!	Embedded Weblinks	Video	EXTRA FEATURES
Identify different types of raccoons. List important features of the raccoon. Compare the similarities and differences between young and adult raccoons. Test your knowledge of raccoons.	Find more information on raccoon identification. Discover more about the history of raccoons. Complete an interactive activity. Get more information on encountering raccoons. Find more raccoon stories and legends.	Watch a video about raccoon behavior. See a raccoon in its natural environment.	**Audio** Listen to sections of the book read aloud. **Key Words** Study vocabulary, and complete a matching word activity. **Slide Show** View images and captions, and prepare a presentation. **Quizzes** Test your knowledge.

AV² was built to bridge the gap between print and digital. We encourage you to tell us what you like and what you want to see in the future.

Sign up to be an AV² Ambassador at www.av2books.com/ambassador.